BIG MONEY IS THE RESULT OF THE EARLIEST START WITH SMALL MONEY

START EARLY WITH A BASIC KNOWLEDGE AND COMPOUND BIG IN A LONG RUN

MUKESH KUMAR

Made with ♥ on the Notion Press Platform
www.notionpress.com

Contents

Foreword *v*

Preface *ix*

Acknowledgements *xi*

1. Investment & Need Of Investment 1
2. Concept Of Financial Market 4
3. Understanding Mutual Fund 14
4. How To Participate Actively In The Stock Market 21

conclusion 43

Foreword

Author Photo

Preface

"The backbone to get financial freedom in your life is the mixture of required amount of financial knowledge at the earliest possible age and earliest start up of the same although with less money."

-MUKESH KUMAR (Author, Financial Advisor, Motivational Speaker and Business Coach)

There is a big gap between literacy rate and financial literacy rate in our country. India is home to around 17 percent population of the world with a literacy rate around 74 percent. And what might come as a surprise is that out of the total population, only 24 percent of the Indian population is financially literate. The 2012 edition of Visa Global Financial Literacy Barometer survey has ranked India at 23rdin a list of 28 countries on the financial literacy front, just ahead of Morocco, South Africa and Vietnam. Brazil as the most financially literate country.

It has been observed that irrespective of availability of money with individuals they are not capable to manage/ mobilise their money in best suitable investment options for a long run to meet major financial requirements and to get the best return on the same to create a big wealth to realise some specific dream in their life only because lack of financial knowledge at early age.

After observing all these facts at the grass root level, It is my heartiest start up to disseminate some required amount of financial knowledge amongst youngsters to fill the gap between money/ saving and proper financial knowledge so that they can mobilise their money in best available investment options at earliest possible age to create a big wealth in the long run to realise their dream in future and finally to get financial freedom.

Acknowledgements

DISCLAIMER

Any advice or information in this is general advice for education purpose only and does not take into account your personal circumstances, please do not trade or invest based solely on this information. By viewing any material or using the information within this book you agree that this is general education material and you will not hold any person or entity responsible for loss or damages resulting from the content or general advice provided here.

Equities, futures, options, and currency trading have large potential rewards, but also large potential risk. You must be aware of the risks and be willing to accept them in order to trade or invest in markets. Don't trade with money you can't afford to lose. The past performance of any trading system or methodology is not necessarily indicative of future results.

Most SEBI registered advisors or the brokerage houses provide stock recommendation with a price target and stop loss but do not share how and what is the basis of such recommendation.

Hence, first try to understand the basis of such recommendation so that with combination of your gained knowledge and regular practice you would be able to take the decision independently.

1

Investment & Need of Investment

The money you earn is partly spent and the rest saved for meeting future expenses. Instead of keeping the savings idle you may like to use savings in order to get return on it in the future. This is called Investment.

One needs to invest to

- Earn return on your idle resources
- Generate a specified sum of money for a specific goal in life
- Make a provision for an uncertain future

When to Start Investing

- The sooner one starts investing the better. By Investing early, you allow your investments more time to grow, increase your income, by accumulating the principal and the interest or dividend earned on it, Year after year.
- *The three golden rules for all investors are:*
  - Invest early
  - Invest regularly
  - Invest for long term and not short term

Where to Invest: One may invest in:

- Physical assets like real estate, gold/jewellery, commodities etc.
- Financial assets such as fixed deposits with banks, small saving instruments with post offices, insurance/provident/pension fund etc or securities market related instruments like shares, bonds, debentures etc.

Short & Long Term Options For Investment

- *Short Term:*
  - Savings Bank Account
  - Money Market or Liquid Funds
  - Fixed Deposit with Banks
- *Long Term:*
  - Post Office Savings
  - Public Provident Fund
  - Bonds
  - Mutual Funds

Equities are considered the most challenging and rewarding, when compared to other investment options.

Research studies have proved that investments in some shares with a longer tenure of investment have yielded far superior returns than any other investment.

However, this does not mean all equity investments would Guarantee similar high returns. Equities are high risk investments. One needs to study them carefully before investing.

According to J.P. Morgan, the following are the 20-year annualised returns by the asset class for 1999-2018: -

- Real Estate Investment trust: 9%
- Gold : 7.75%
- Oil : 7%
- Nifty: 12%
- Bonds : 4.5%
- Homes : 3.4%

Power of Compounding:

The power of compounding works by growing your wealth exponentially. It adds the profit earned back to the principal amount and then reinvests the entire sum to accelerate the profit earning process.

As per below mentioned table- Suppose, you invest ? 1000 per month on estimated CAGR of 15% per annum. Your investment becomes ? 13800/- after the first year, then ? 29670/- after 2nd year and ? 1413721.44/- after twenty years on your principally invested money of ? 240000/- only.

- This calculation is enough to understand the meaning of the name of this book.
- It also shows that if these small investment habits are taken on time by the every guardian and pass the same to next generations then the outcome will serve a great purpose in the life of an adult at the stage of most needed requirements of money.

- After exercising these small investment habits with less money but in continuity, no guardians will feel burdensome to meet a big required money for their children in the age of their 20s for their higher education or for any other great purpose.

- In the matter of girls, it will work as a safety and security for them and encourage them enough to take any bold step to attain freedom from all aspects of evils of the society.

Now after observing all these facts, you are smart enough to understand the value of investment at the right age.
YearAt Starting yearAnnual subsAt the end of the yearCAGRAnnual Profit

1	1000	12	12000	15%	1800
2	13800	12000	25800	15%	3870
3	29670	12000	41670	15%	6250.5
4	47920.5	12000	59920.5	15%	8988.075
5	68908.575	12000	80908.575	15%	12136.28625
6	93044.86125	12000	105044.8613	15%	15756.72919
7	120801.5904	12000	132801.5904	15%	19920.23857
8	152721.829	12000	164721.829	15%	24708.27435
9	189430.1034	12000	201430.1034	15%	30214.5155
10	231644.6189	12000	243644.6189	15%	36546.69283
11	280191.3117	12000	292191.3117	15%	43828.69675
12	336020.0084	12000	348020.0084	15%	52203.00127
13	400223.0097	12000	412223.0097	15%	61833.45146
14	474056.4612	12000	486056.4612	15%	72908.46917
15	558964.9303	12000	570964.9303	15%	85644.73955
16	656609.6699	12000	668609.6699	15%	100291.4505
17	768901.1204	12000	780901.1204	15%	117135.1681
18	898036.2884	12000	910036.2884	15%	136505.4433
19	1046541.732	12000	1058541.732	15%	158781.2598
20	1217322.991	12000	1229322.991	15%	184398.4487
21	1413721.44				
22					
23			12000	20	240000

2

Concept of Financial Market

A business is a part of an economic System that consists of two main sectors – households which save Funds and business firms which Invest these funds. A financial market Helps to link the savers and the Investors by mobilizing funds between Them. There are two major alternative mechanisms through which allocation of funds can be done: via banks or via financial markets. Households can deposit their surplus funds with banks, who in turn could lend these funds to business firms. Alternately, households can buy the shares and debentures offered by a business using financial markets.

Banks and financial markets are competing Intermediaries in the financial system and give households a choice of where They want to place their savings.

Functions of Financial Market:

- Mobilisation of Savings and Channelling them into the most Productive Uses: A financial market Facilitates the transfer of savings from Savers to investors. It gives savers the Choice of different investments and Thus helps to channelise surplus funds into the most productive use.
- Facilitating Price Discovery: You All know that the forces of demand and supply help to establish a price for a commodity or service in the Market. In the financial market, the Households are suppliers of funds and Business firms represent the demand. The interaction between them helps to establish a price for the financial Asset which is being traded in that Particular market.
- Providing Liquidity to Financial Assets: Financial markets facilitate easy purchase and sale of financial assets. In doing so they provide liquidity to financial assets, so that they can be easily converted into cash whenever required. Holders of assets can readily sell them financial assets through the mechanism of the financial market.
- Less time-consuming and cost-effective as parties don't have to spend extra time and money to find potential clients to deal with securities. It also decreases cost by giving valuable information about the securities traded in the financial market.
- Reducing the Cost of Transactions: Financial markets provide valuable information about securities being traded in the market. It helps to save time, effort and money that both buyers and sellers of a financial asset would have to otherwise spend to try and find each other. The financial market is thus a common platform where buyers and sellers can meet for fulfilment of their individual needs.

Types of Financial Markets:

- Over the Counter (OTC) Market – They manage public stock exchanges, which are not listed on the NASDAQ, American Stock Exchange, and New York Stock Exchange. The OTC market dealing with companies are usually small companies that can be traded cheaply and have less regulation.

- Bond Market – A financial market is a place where investors loan money on bonds as security for a set of time at a predefined rate of interest. Bonds are issued by corporations, states, municipalities, and federal governments across the world.

- Money Markets – They trade high liquid and short maturities, and lending of securities that matures in less than a year.
- Derivatives Market –They trade securities that determine its value from its primary asset. The derivative contract value is regulated by the market price of the primary item — the derivatives market securities, including futures, options, contracts-for- difference, forward contracts, and swaps.
- Forex Market – It is a financial market where investors trade in currencies. In the entire world, this is the most liquid financial market.

Classification of Financial Market:

The financial market can be classified into three different forms.

- ### *By Nature of Claim:*

    - Debt Market – It is a market where fixed bonds and debentures, or bonds are exchanged between investors.
    - Equity Market – It is a place for investors to deal with equity.

- ### *By Maturity of Claim:*

    - Money Market – It deals with monetary assets and short-term funds such as a certificate of deposits, treasury bills, and commercial paper, etc. which mature within twelve months.
    - Capital Market – It trades medium and long-term financial assets.

- ### *By Timing of Delivery:*

    - Cash Market – It is a marketplace where trade is completed in real-time.
    - Futures Market – Here, the delivery or compensation of products are taken on the future specified date.

- ### *By Organizational Structure:*

    - Exchange-Traded Market – It has a centralised system with a patterned procedure.
    - Over-the-Counter Market – It has a decentralised organisation with customised procedures.

We will study Financial markets particularly classified on the basis of the maturity of financial instruments traded in them.

- Instruments with a maturity of less than one year are traded in the money market.
- Instruments with longer maturity are traded in the capital market.

Money Market:

- It is a market where low risk, unsecured and short-term debt instruments that are highly liquid are issued and actively traded every day. It has no physical location, but is an activity conducted over the telephone and through the internet. It enables the raising of short- term funds for meeting the temporary shortages of cash and obligations and the temporary deployment of excess funds for earning returns. The major participants in the market are the Reserve Bank of India (RBI), Commercial Banks, Non-Banking Finance Companies,State Governments, Large Corporate Houses and Mutual Funds. Money Market Instruments

Treasury Bill:

- A Treasury bill is basically an instrument of short- term borrowing by the Government of India maturing in less than one year. They are also known as Zero Coupon Bonds Issued by the Reserve Bank of India on behalf of the Central Government To meet its short-term requirement of funds. Treasury bills are issued in the form of a promissory note. They are highly liquid and have assured yield and negligible risk of default. They are issued at a price which is lower than their face value and repaid at par. the difference between the price at which the treasury bills are Issued and their redemption value is the interest receivable on them and Is called discount. Treasury bills are available for a minimum amount of `25,000 and in multiples thereof.
- Example: Suppose an investor Purchases a 91 days Treasury bill with a face value of ` 1,00,000 for `96,000. By holding the bill until the maturity date, the investor receives `1,00,000. The difference of `4,000 Between the proceeds received at maturity and the amount paid to purchase the bill represents the Interest received by him.

Commercial Paper:

- Commercial Paper is a short-term unsecured Promissory note, negotiable and transferable by endorsement and delivery with a fixed maturity period. It is issued by large and creditworthy Companies to raise short-term funds at lower rates of interest than market rates. It usually has a maturity period of 15 days to one year. The issuance of commercial paper is an alternative to bank borrowing for large companies That are generally considered to be financially strong. It is sold at a discount and redeemed at par. The original purpose of commercial paper was to provide short-terms funds for seasonal and working capital Needs. For example, companies use This instrument for purposes such as bridge financing.
- Example: Suppose a company needs long-term finance to buy some machinery. In order to raise the long-term funds in the capital market the company will have to incur Floatation costs (costs associated with Floating of an issue are brokerage, Commission, printing of applications and advertising, etc.). Funds raised through commercial paper are used to meet the floatation costs. This is known as Bridge Financing.

Call Money:

- Call money is short term finance repayable on demand, with a maturity period of one day to fifteen days, used for inter-bank transactions. Commercial banks must maintain a minimum cash balance known as cash reserve ratio. The Reserve Bank of India changes the cash reserve ratio from time to time which in turn affects the amount of funds available to be given as loans by commercial banks. Call Money is a method by which banks borrow from each other to be able to maintain the cash reserve ratio. The interest rate paid on call money loans is known as the call rate. It is a highly volatile rate that varies from day-to-day and sometimes even from hour-to-hour. There is an inverse relationship between call rates and other short-term money market instruments such as certificates of deposit and commercial paper. A rise in call money rates makes other sources of finance such as commercial paper and certificates of deposit cheaper in comparison for banks to raise funds from these sources.

Certificate of Deposit:

- Certificates of deposit (CD) are unsecured, negotiable, short-term instruments in bearer form, issued by commercial banks and development financial institutions. They can be issued to individuals, corporations and companies during periods of tight liquidity when the deposit growth of banks is slow but the demand for credit is high. They help to mobilise a large amount of money for short periods.

Commercial Bill:

- A commercial bill is a bill of exchange used to finance the working capital requirements of business firms. It is a short-term, negotiable, self-liquidating instrument which is used to finance the credit sales of firms. When goods are sold on credit, the buyer becomes liable to make payment on a specific date in future. The seller could wait till the specified date or make use of a bill of exchange. The seller (drawer) of the goods draws the bill and the buyer (drawee) accepts it. On being accepted, the bill becomes a marketable instrument and is called a trade bill. These bills can be discounted with a bank if the seller needs funds before the bill matures. When a trade bill is accepted by a commercial bank it is known as a commercial bill.

Capital Market:

- The term capital market refers to Facilities and institutional arrangements Through which long-term funds, both debt and equity are raised and Invested. In other words, Capital markets are venues where savings and investments are channelled between the suppliers who have capital and those who are in need of capital. The entities that have capital include retail and institutional investors while those who seek capital are businesses, governments, and people.

Capital Market – Structure:

- Capital markets structure is made of primary and secondary markets.

Primary markets

- Primary markets consist of companies that issue securities and investors who purchase those securities directly from the issuing company. These securities are called Initial Public Offerings (IPO). The investors in this market are banks, financial institutions, insurance companies, mutual funds and individuals.

  There are various methods of floating New issues in the primary market:
  Offer through Prospectus:

- Offer Through prospectus is the most popular method of raising funds by public Companies in the primary market. This involves inviting subscriptions from the public through the issue of Prospectus. A prospectus makes a Direct appeal to investors to raise Capital, through an advertisement in newspapers and magazines. The Issues may be underwritten and are required to be listed on at least one Stock exchange. The contents of the Prospectus have to be in accordance with the provisions of the Companies Act and SEBI disclosure and investor Protection guidelines.

  Offer for Sale:

- Under this method Securities are not issued directly to the Public but are offered for sale through Intermediaries like issuing houses or Stock brokers. In this case, a company Sells securities in bloc at an agreed price to brokers who, in turn, resell them to the investing public.

  Private Placement:

- Private Placement is the allotment of securities by a company to institutional investors and some selected individuals. It Helps to raise capital more quickly Than a public issue. Access to the Primary market can be expensive on account of various mandatory and non- mandatory expenses. Some Companies, therefore, cannot afford a Public issue and choose to use private Placement.

  Rights Issue:

- This is a privilege given to existing shareholders to subscribe to a new issue of shares according to the terms and conditions of the company.

Secondary markets

- Secondary marketsare places where the trade of already issued certificates between investors are overseen by regulatory bodies. Issuing companies play no part in the secondary market. It helps existing investors to disinvest and fresh Investors to enter the market. Examples of secondary markets are New York Stock Exchange (NYSE), London Stock Exchange (LSE), Bombay Stock Exchange (BSE).

Primary and Secondary Markets — A Comparison

Primary Market (New Issue Market)

1. There is sale of securities by new Companies or further (new issues of Securities by existing companies to Investors).
2. Securities are sold by the company to the investor directly (or through an intermediary).
3. The flow of funds is from savers to Investors, i.e. the primary market Directly promotes capital formation.
4. Only buying of securities takes place in the primary market, securities cannot be sold there.
5. Prices are determined and decided by the management of the company.
6. There is no fixed geographical location.

Secondary Market (Stock Exchange)

1. There is trading of existing shares only.
2. Ownership of existing securities is Exchanged between investors. The Company is not involved at all.
3. Enhances encash ability (liquidity) Of shares, i.e. the secondary market Indirectly promotes capital formation.
4. Both the buying and the selling of Securities can take place on the Stock Exchange.
5. Prices are determined by demand and supply for the security.
6. Located at specific places.

- Securities are traded, cleared and Settled within the regulatory framework Prescribed by SEBI. Advances in Information technology have made Trading through stock exchanges accessible from anywhere in the Country through trading terminals.
- Along with the growth of the Primary Market in the country, the Secondary Market has also grown significantly during the last ten years.

Stock Exchange:

- A stock exchange is an institution which provides a platform for buying and selling of existing securities. As a market, the stock exchange facilitates the exchange of a security (share, debenture etc.) into money and vice versa. Stock exchanges help Companies raise finance, provide liquidity and safety of investment to the investors and enhance the credit worthiness of individual companies.

  The following are Some of the important functions of a Stock exchange.

- Providing Liquidity and Marketability to Existing Securities: The basic function of a stock exchange is the creation of a continuous market where Securities are bought and sold. It gives Investors the chance to disinvest and reinvest. This provides both liquidity and easy marketability to already existing securities in the market.

- Pricing of Securities: Share prices on a stock exchange are determined by the forces of demand and supply. A stock exchange is a mechanism of Constant valuation through which the prices of securities are determined. Such a valuation provides important Instant information to both buyers and sellers in the market.

- Safety of Transaction: The membership of a stock exchange is well regulated, and its dealings are well defined according to the existing legal framework. This ensures that the investing public gets a safe and fair deal on the market.
- Contributes to Economic Growth: A stock exchange is a market in which existing securities are resold or traded. Through this process of disinvestment and reinvestment savings get channelised into their most productive investment avenues. This leads to capital formation and economic growth.
- Spreading of Equity Cult: The stock exchange can play a vital role in ensuring wider share ownership by regulating new issues, better trading practices and taking effective steps in educating the public about investments.
- Providing Scope for Speculation: The stock exchange provides sufficient scope within the provisions of law for speculative activity in a restricted and controlled manner. It is generally accepted that a certain degree of healthy speculation is necessary to ensure liquidity and price continuity in the stock market.

A stock exchange has its Main computer system with many Terminals spread across the country. Trading in securities is done through Brokers who are members of the stock Exchange. Trading has shifted from the Stock market floor to the brokers office.

Every broker has to have access to A computer terminal that is connected to the main stock exchange. In this Screen-based trading, a member logs on to the site and any information about the shares (company, member, etc.) he wishes to buy or sell, and the price is fed into the computer. The software is so designed that the transaction will be executed when a matching order is found from a counter party. The whole transaction is carried on the computer Screen with both the parties being able to see the prices of all shares going up and down at all times during the time that business is transacted and during business hours of the stock exchange. The computer in the brokers office is constantly matching the orders at the best bid and offer price. Those that are not matched remain on the screen and are open for future matching during the day.

Now, screen-based trading or on-line trading is the only way in which you can buy or sell shares. Shares can be held either in physical form or an electronic book entry form of holding and transferring shares can also be adopted. This electronic form is called dematerialised form.

Depository:

- Just like a bank keeps money in safe custody for customers, a depository also is like a bank and keeps securities in electronic form on behalf of the Investor. In India, there are two depositories.
- National Securities Depositories Limited (NSDL) is the first and largest Depository presently operational in India. It was promoted as a joint Venture of the IDBI, UTI, and the National Stock Exchange.
- The Central Depository Services Limited (CDSL) is the second Depository to commence operations and was promoted by the Bombay Stock Exchange and the Bank of India.
- Both these national level depositories Operate through intermediaries who are electronically connected to the Depository and serve as contact points with the investors and are called Depository participants. The Depository Participant (DP) Serves as an intermediary between the Investor and the Depository (NSDL or CDSL) who is authorised to maintain the accounts of dematerialised shares. Financial institutions, banks, clearing Corporations, stock brokers and Non-banking finance corporations are permitted to become Depository Participants.

If the investor is buying and selling the securities through the Broker or the bank or a non-banking Finance corporation, it acts as a DP for the investor and completes the formalities.

The National Stock Exchange

- The National Stock Exchange is the latest, most modern and technology driven exchange. It was incorporated in 1992 and was recognised as a Stock Exchange in April 1993. it started operations in 1994, with trading on the wholesale debt market segment. Subsequently, it launched the capital market segment in November 1994 as a trading platform for equities and the futures and options segment in June 2000 for various derivative instruments. NSE has set up a nationwide fully automated screen-based trading system.
- It has provided a nationwide screen based automated trading system with a high degree of transparency and equal access to investors irrespective of geographical location.

BSE Ltd (formerly known as Bombay Stock Exchange Ltd)

- The BSE Ltd was established in 1875 and was Asia's first Stock Exchange. It was granted permanent recognition under the Securities Contract (Regulation) Act, 1956. It has contributed to the growth of the corporate sector by providing a platform for raising capital. It is known as BSE Ltd but was established as the Native Share Stock Brokers Association in 1875. Even before the actual legislations were enacted, BSE Ltd already had a set of Rules and Regulations to ensure an orderly growth of the securities market.

Objectives:

- Establishing a nationwide trading facility for all types of securities.
- Ensuring equal access to investors all over the country through an appropriate communication Network.
- Providing a fair, efficient and transparent securities market using electronic trading system.
- Enabling shorter settlement cycles and book entry settlements.
- Meeting international benchmarks and standards

Stock Market Index:

- A stock market index is a barometer of market behaviour. It measures overall market sentiment through a set of stocks that are representative of the market. It reflects market direction and indicates day-to-day fluctuations in stock prices. An ideal index must represent changes in the prices of securities and reflect price movements of typical shares for better market representation. In the Indian markets The BSE, SENSEX and NSE, NIFTY are important indices. Some important global stock market indices are:-
- Dow Jones Industrial average is among the oldest quoted stock market index in the US.
- NASDAQ Composite Index is the market capitalisation weightages of prices for Stocks listed in the NASDAQ stock market.
- S & P 500 Index is made up of 500 biggest publicly traded companies in the US. The S & P 500 is often treated as a proxy for the US stock market.
- FTSE 100 consists of the largest 100 companies by full market value listed On the London Stock Exchange. The FTSE 100 is the benchmark index of the European market.

BULLS and BEARS –

- The term does not refer to animals but to market sentiment of the investors.

PENNY STOCKS –

- These are securities that have no value on the stock exchange but Whose trading contributes to speculation.

Securities and Exchange Board of India (SEBI):

- The Securities and Exchange Board of India was established by the Government of India on 12 April 1988 as an interim administrative body to promote orderly and healthy growth of the securities market and for Investor protection. It was to function under the overall administrative control of the Ministry of Finance of The Government of India.
- The SEBI Was given statutory status on 30 January 1992 through an ordinance. The ordinance was later replaced by an Act of Parliament known as the Securities and Exchange Board of India Act, 1992.

Reasons for the Establishment of SEBI:

- The capital market has witnessed a tremendous growth during 1980's, Characterised particularly by the increasing participation of the Public. These ever-expanding investors Population and market capitalisation led to a variety of malpractices on the part of companies, brokers, merchant bankers, investment consultants and others involved in the securities market. The glaring examples of these malpractices include existence of self-styled merchant bankers, unofficial Private placements, rigging of prices, unofficial premium on new issues, non-adherence of provisions of the Companies Act, violation of rules and regulations of stock exchanges and listing requirements, delay in delivery of shares etc. These malpractices and unfair trading practices have eroded Investor confidence and multiplied Investor grievances.

The Government and the stock exchanges were rather helpless in redressing the investor's problems because of lack of proper penal provisions in the existing legislation. In view of the above, the Government of India decided to set-up a separate regulatory body known as Securities and Exchange Board of India.

Purpose and Role of SEBI:

- The basic purpose of SEBI is to create an environment to facilitate efficient mobilisation and allocation of resources through the securities markets. It also aims to stimulate competition and encourage innovation. This environment includes rules and regulations, institutions and their interrelationships, instruments, practices, infrastructure and policy framework. This environment aims at meeting the needs of the three groups which basically constitute the market, viz, the issuers of securities (Companies), the investors and the market intermediaries.
- To the issuers, it aims to provide a marketplace in which they can confidently look forward to raising finances they need in an easy, fair and efficient manner.
- To the investors, it should provide protection of their rights and interests through adequate, accurate and authentic information and disclosure of information on a continuous basis.
- To the intermediaries, it should offer a competitive, professionalised and expanding market with adequate and efficient infrastructure so that they are able to render better service to the investors and issuers.

Objectives of SEBI:

- The overall objective of SEBI is to protect the interests of investors and to promote the development of and regulate the securities market. SEBI has been restructured and Rationalised in tune with its expanded scope. It has decided its activities into Five operational departments. Each Department is headed by an executive Director. Apart from its head office at Mumbai, SEBI has opened regional Offices in Kolkata, Chennai, and Delhi to attend to investor complaints and liaise with the issuers, intermediaries and stock exchanges in the concerned Region.

The SEBI also formed two advisory Committees. They are the Primary Market Advisory Committee and The Secondary Market Advisory Committee.

These committees consist of the market players, the investors Associations recognised by the SEBI and the eminent persons in the capital Market. They provide important inputs to the SEBI's policies.

The objectives of the two Committees are as follows:

- To advise SEBI on matters relating to the regulation of intermediaries for ensuring investors protection in the primary market.
- To advise SEBI on issues related to the development of primary market In India.
- To advise SEBI on disclosure requirements for companies.
- To advise for changes in legal framework to Introduce simplification and transparency in the primary market.
- To advise the board in matters relating to the development and regulation of the secondary market in the country.
- The committees are however non-Statutory in nature and the SEBI is not bound by the advice of the committee. These committees are a part of SEBI's Constant endeavour to obtain feedback from the market players on various Issues relating to the regulations and development of the market.

How to participate in the Stock market?

There are broadly two way to participate/ invest in stock market: -

- Through Active Participation: You directly purchase/ sell equities, securities or eligible financial instruments as per your own assessment through direct participation.
- Through Mutual Fund: Through opening an account with AMC (Asset Management Company) where Portfolio managers take decisions as per your investment objectives.

3

Understanding Mutual Fund

"Mutual Fund investments are subject to market risks, read all scheme related documents carefully."

Probably all of you read or listened to this sentence while watching TVs or reading magazines.

So, let's have a look to understand the whole story behind it.

Mutual Fund Basics:

- A Mutual Fund is a *financial intermediary/ trust*, set up with an objective to professionally manage the money pooled from the investors at large.
- An investor in a mutual fund scheme receives units which are in accordance with the quantum of money invested by him. These units represent an investor's proportionate ownership into the assets of a scheme and his liability in case of loss to the fund is limited to the extent of the amount invested by him.
- Mutual funds provide the benefit of professional management as people's money is managed by experienced fund managers. However, these decisions are governed by certain guidelines which are decided by the investment objective(s), investment pattern of the scheme and are subject to regulatory restrictions. It is this investment objective and investment pattern which also guides the investor in choosing the right fund for his investment purpose.
- Today, there are a variety of schemes offered by mutual funds in India, which cater to different categories of investors to suit different financial objectives e.g. some schemes may provide capital protection for the risk-averse investor, whereas some other schemes may provide for capital appreciation by investing in mid or small cap segment of the equity market for the more aggressive investor.

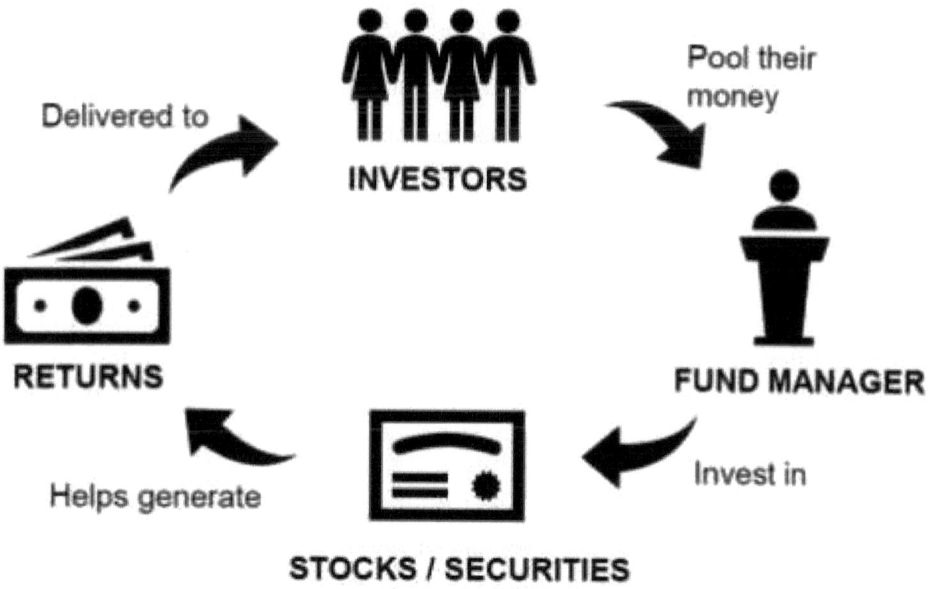

Mutual Fund Functioning Representation

How are Mutual Funds set up?

A mutual fund is set up in the form of a trust, which has Sponsor, Trustees, Asset Management Company (AMC) and Custodian. The trust is established by a sponsor or more than one sponsor who is like a promoter of a company and registered with Securities and Exchange Board of India (SEBI). Asset Management Company (AMC) approved by SEBI manages the funds by making investments in various types of securities.

Benefits of Mutual Fund

There are two major reasons why most people around the globe are afraid to make investment decisions on their own. One of them is the lack of time to study the pros and cons of different investment opportunities and the other being lack of financial know-how. Apart from that Investment needs across different categories of investors are also not common. While some may settle for safety of capital, others may chase returns. There may be others who would want their capital to grow at a steady pace, while some may want to save for retirement or child's education. The needs and objectives of the investors are truly diverse and one financial product can't fulfil all of them. The emergence of mutual funds in the past decade as a popular investment vehicle is due to the fact that it serves broadly all categories of investors through the plethora of schemes that it offers. The benefits provided by mutual funds far outweigh its shortcomings and has thus gained wide-spread acceptance.

Following are the key benefits of investing in mutual funds:

Professional Management:

- Mutual funds provide the benefit of professional management as people's money is managed by experienced fund managers. Investors, who do not have time, inclination and the know-how to manage their investments, can look towards mutual funds as an alternative. It is inexpensive and is ideal for a small ticket investor.

- Diversification: Mutual funds provide investors with the benefit of diversification across different companies and sectors. Diversification in simple terms means to spread your portfolio across different instruments, sectors, industries, companies and countries so that the overall portfolio is relatively safeguarded from downturns in one or more sectors, companies or countries. Since small investors do not have enough money to make meaningful investments across different assets, a mutual fund does the job for them.
- Liquidity: Open ended mutual funds provide easy liquidity and investors can buy or sell units anytime, at the prevailing NAV based prices. Close-ended schemes are listed on a stock exchange where investors can redeem their units at the prevailing market price. Interval funds which are a cross between a close-ended and an open-ended structure also provide periodic liquidity options to its investors.
- Flexibility: There are a lot of features in a regular mutual fund scheme, which imparts flexibility to the scheme. An investor can opt for a Systematic Investment Plan (SIP), Systematic Withdrawal Plan (SWP), Systematic Transfer Plan (STP)etc. to plan his cash flow requirements as per his convenience. The wide range of schemes being launched in India by different mutual funds also provides an added flexibility to the investor to build his portfolio accordingly.
- Convenience: Mutual fund companies offer convenient routes to investing in their schemes. Investors can invest through the internet or mobile phone in addition to the conventional option of physically filling up an application form and submitting it. Further, as bank details are required to be submitted at the time of investment, redemptions become very convenient as an investor directly receives the proceeds in the bank account.
- Transparency: The mutual fund industry in India works on a very transparent basis, and various kinds of information is available to their investors through fact sheets, offer documents, annual reports etc.
- Well Regulated: The Indian Mutual Fund industry is well regulated by the Securities and Exchange Board of India (SEBI). This helps to instil confidence and provides comfort to the investors. The regulatory environment in India is quite healthy and ensures transparency in the processes and transactions. The best practices adopted by the industry in India have helped them win investors' confidence over the years. The ease and convenience which mutual funds offer, and the different variety of schemes made available to the investors creates popularity for mutual funds, which cuts across investor classes and creates a favourable appeal.

Types of Mutual Fund Schemes:

A mutual fund scheme can be classified into an open-ended scheme or close-ended scheme depending on its maturity period.

- Open-ended Fund/Scheme: An open-ended fund or scheme is one that is available for subscription and repurchase on a continuous basis. These schemes do not have a fixed maturity period. Investors can conveniently buy and sell units at Net Asset Value (NAV) per unit which is declared on a daily basis. The key feature of open-end schemes is liquidity.
- Close-ended Fund/Sche*me:* A close-ended fund or scheme has a stipulated maturity period e.g. 3-5 years. The fund is open for subscription only during a specified period at the time of launch of the scheme. Investors can invest in the scheme at the time of the new fund offer and thereafter they can buy or sell the units of the scheme on the stock exchanges where the units are listed. In order to provide an exit route to the investors, some close-ended funds give an option of selling back the units to the mutual fund through periodic repurchases at NAV related prices. SEBI Regulations stipulate that at least one of the two exit routes are provided to the investor i.e. either repurchase facility or through listing on stock exchanges.

Classification based on investment objective:

Apart from the above classification, mutual fund schemes can also be classified based on their investment objectives.

- Equity Funds: Growth/ Equity oriented schemes are those schemes which predominantly invest in equity and equity related instruments. The objective of such schemes is to provide *capitalappreciationoverthemediumtolongterm.* These types of schemes are generally meant for investors with a long-term investment horizon and with a higher risk appetite.

Type of Equity Funds

Diversified Funds:-

- Multi-Cap Funds: These funds invest across the market capitalization i.e. in large, mid and small cap companies.
- Large Cap: These funds invest predominantly in large companies. Generally, large cap companies experience a slower growth rate and have much lower risk than mid cap companies due to their size. They are *alsoknownasbluechipcompanies.*
- Mid Cap: These funds invest predominantly in mid cap companies. Most mid cap companies experience higher growth than a large cap company.
- Small Cap: Small cap refers to a company that is relatively new and has lower market capitalisation. Of the three, small cap companies represent the most investment risk but also the highest return potential.

Tax Saving Fund:

- These funds are also known as Equity Linked Savings Schemes (ELSS). In case of ELSS schemes investment upto Rs. 1 lakh qualify for deductions under Section 80C of the Income tax Act, 1961, however, these schemes have a lock in period of 3 years.

Equity–International:

- These funds invest in companies of foreign countries. The investment could be specific to a country (like the China, US fund etc.) or diversified across countries/ regions (like Europe, Asia etc.). By seeking exposure to foreign stocks in a portfolio one can spread investment risk and achieve diversification. AMCs generally tie up with a foreign fund (called 'Underlying Fund') and in India they launch a 'Feeder Fund'. The money collected in the feeder fund is invested in the underlying fund. Sometimes AMCs also launch schemes investing directly in equity securities of international companies. In such schemes, the local investors invest in rupees for buying the units. The rupees are converted into foreign currency for investing abroad. Thus, there is an element of foreign currency risk while investing in such schemes. Also, it should be noted that tax treatment of international equity funds is similar to debt funds.

Equity Income / Dividend Yield Schemes:

- Dividend yield schemes generally invest in a well-diversified portfolio of companies with relatively high dividend yield, which provides a steady stream of cash flows by way of dividend.

Sector Funds:

- Sector funds invest in companies in a particular sector. For example, a banking sector fund will invest only in shares of banking companies.

Thematic funds:

- Thematic Funds invest in line with an investment theme. For example, an infrastructure thematic fund will invest in shares of companies that are directly or indirectly related to the infrastructure sector.

Arbitrage Funds:

- These funds exploit arbitrage opportunities such that the risk is neutralized, but a return is earned. The arbitrage is sought by taking advantage of a price differential of the same asset between two or more markets, say, taking advantage of the mispricing between the cash and derivatives market. These funds generally have low risk-return trade-off.

Index Funds :

- Index Funds invests in companies that constitute the index and in the same proportion, in order to replicate a specific market index and provide a rate of return over time that will approximate or match that of the market which they are mirroring, subject to tracking error.

Income/ Debt Oriented Funds:

- Such schemes generally invest in debt securities like Treasury Bills, Government Securities, Bonds and Debentures etc. They are considered less risky than equity schemes, but also offer lower returns.

Gilt Funds:

- These funds invest exclusively in Government securities. Government securities have no default risk. NAVs of these schemes also fluctuate due to changes in interest rates and other economic factors as is the case with income or debt-oriented schemes.

Money Market/Liquid Funds:

- These funds aim to provide easy liquidity, preservation of capital and moderate income. They invest in safer short-term instruments such as certificates of deposit, commercial paper, etc. These schemes are used mainly by institutions and individuals to park their surplus funds for short periods of time. These funds are more or less insulated from changes in the interest rate in the economy and capture the current yields prevailing in the market.

Hybrid Funds/ Balanced Funds:

- These are the funds that aim at allocating the total assets within the portfolio *mixofdebtandequityinstruments.* Balanced funds provide investors with an option of a single mutual fund that combines both growth and income objectives, by investing in both stocks (for growth) and bonds (for income). Balanced funds are also called equity-oriented funds and their tax treatment is similar to an equity fund. Their average returns and risk profile fall somewhere in between growth and debt funds.

Investment Plans/Options available to investors

Investment Plans

1. Direct plan:

SEBI has mandated mutual funds to compulsorily launch a direct plan for direct investments, i.e., investments not routed through a distributor, from 01 January 2013. Such a separate plan has a lower expense ratio excluding distribution expenses, commission, etc., and no commission is to be paid from such plans. The plan also has a separate NAV.

Investment can be made in lump sum, i.e. a onetime payment, or through a Systematic Investment Plan (SIP).

What is a Systematic Investment Plan (SIP)?

A SIP allows an investor to invest regularly. One puts in a small amount every month that is invested in a mutual fund. A SIP allows one to take part in the stock market without trying to second-guess its movements.

2. Regular or Normal Plan:

- Under regular or normal plan investors can invest through an agent or distributor in order to avail their investment advice/services. The regular plan too has a separate NAV, which is generally lower than direct plan as the former charges higher expenses in order to pay commission to an intermediary involved.

Investment Options

- Growth Option: Under growth option, dividends are not paid out to the unit holders. Income attributable to the unit holders continues to remain invested in the scheme and is reflected in the NAV of units under this option.

Investors can realize capital appreciation if any, by way of an increase in NAV of their units by redeeming them.

- Dividend Pay-out Option: Dividends are paid out to the unit holders under this option. However, the NAV of the units falls to the extent of the dividend paid out and applicable statutory levies.
- Dividend Re-investment Option: The dividend that accrues on units under option is re-invested back into the scheme at ex- dividend NAV. Hence investors receive additional units on their investments in lieu of dividends.

Some Informative Points:

What is the Net Asset Value (NAV) of a scheme?

- NAV is the market value of the securities held by the scheme. Since the market value of securities changes every day, the NAV of a scheme also varies on a day to day basis. The NAV per unit is the market value of securities of a scheme divided by the total number of units of the scheme on any particular date. For example, if the market value of securities of a mutual fund scheme is INR 200 lakh and the mutual fund has issued 10 lakh units of INR 10 each to the investors, then the NAV per unit of the fund is INR 20 (i.e.200 lakh/10 lakh). NAV is required to be disclosed by the mutual funds on a daily basis.
- The NAV per unit of all mutual fund schemes have to be updated on AMFI's website and the Mutual Funds' website by 9 p.m. of the same day. Fund of Funds are allowed time till 10 a.m. the following business day to update the information.
- Demat account is required for MF investments: Except in case of schemes which are listed on the stock exchange and are available on their platforms, demat account is not required to own units in a mutual fund scheme.
- Fees and Expenses: As is the case with any other business, running a mutual fund business also involves costs. The various costs incurred by a mutual fund could be associated with transactions made by investors, operating costs, marketing and distribution expenses etc. Expenses borne by the mutual fund investor can be broadly classified into two categories: -

i. The load which may be charged to the investor at the time of redemption
ii. The recurring expenses which are charged to the fund.

- Loads or Sales Charges: Loads are charges which investors incur when they redeem units in a mutual fund scheme. A load charged at the time of redemption is known as 'Exit Load or Back End Load'. Asset management companies charge these loads to defray the selling and distribution expenses including commission paid to the agents/ distributors. Since August 1, 2009 entry load has been banned and therefore purchase/subscription of mutual funds happen at a price which is equal to the NAV. However, an investor is required to pay an exit load (if any) if he chooses to redeem units. This happens at a price linked to the NAV.
- Recurring Expenses: These are costs incurred for day to day operation of a scheme. These expenses inter alia include investment management and advisory fees, trustee fees, registrar's fees, custodian's fees, Audit fees, marketing and selling expenses including agents' commission etc. Expenses exceeding the specified limit are to be borne by the AMC.

4

How to Participate Actively in the Stock Market

Through Active Participation:

Now we will discuss how to participate actively in the stock market: -

Basic Trading Concepts:

Fundamental and Technical Analysis : Fundamental analysis and technical analysis are the two broad, general approaches to market analysis and trading. Each approach has its advocates and its detractors, and there are hugely successful – and unsuccessful – traders in both camps.

**Fundamental market Analysts*

- Fundamental market Analysts attempt to identify a stock or other security's intrinsic Value by looking at factors such as overall economic conditions, Industry trends, company management, profit and loss data, and Any of a number of financial metrics that are used to determine the Financial health and future prospects for a company. Some of the Most commonly used financial metrics are the price-to-earnings Ratio (P/E), price-to-book ratio (P/B), debt-to- equity ratio(D/E), return On investment (ROI), and return on assets (ROA).
- Fundamental stock traders rely heavily on data such as a Company's quarterly and annual earnings reports, to see the Earnings-per-share which indicates a company's profitability as Divided among the total amount of publicly traded equity in the Company. Additional data for analysis by fundamental traders is Gleaned from the published financial statements of publicly traded Companies, such as a company's income statement and balance Sheet.
- The exact nature of fundamental analysis varies according to Investments. For example, fundamental traders of the foreign Exchange – forex – market eye data such as gross domestic product (GDP), manufacturing, import and export data, and the consumer Price index (CPI) in order to assess the overall health of a nation's Economy. Logically, nations with stronger economies will also likely Have relatively stronger currencies.
- Advocates of fundamental analysis point out that it is based on Solid financial data, and therefore likely to be reliable. However, a drawback of fundamental analysis is that it requires time-consuming research and doing things like financial modelling and company valuations is not an endeavour well-suited to many investors.

**Technical Market Analysts*

- Technical analysts ignore all the factors considered by fundamental analysts, and instead concentrate their evaluation of a security solely on analysing market price action in order to identify current and likely future price trends. The basic belief of technical traders is that all relevant factors of supply and demand are reflected in the price movement of a security.

- Technical traders argue, for example, that there's no need to engage in the practice of fundamental traders attempting to assess whether current economic or marketplace conditions favour increasing demand for a company's products – Instead, technical traders would say that if the company's stock price is rising steadily, then that shows that their products are in increasing demand.

- The basic tool of technical analysts is the price chart. Technical analysts look at all manner of data that can be plotted on a price chart for a security, such as trend lines, trading volume, moving averages, and support and resistance levels.

- Technical analysts don't bother attempting to identify intrinsic value of s security, instead using chart analysis to identify price action patterns that indicate probable future price direction and movement.

- Both the strength and the weakness of technical analysis lie in the fact that there is virtually an endless list of technical indicators to choose from in analysing a security.

So, Which One Should You Use – Fundamental or Technical Analysis?

Answer is Your personal preference and what is best suited to your personal trading style, financial goals, and risk tolerance. The practical fact is that while 50 or 100 years ago fundamental Analysis held sway, the arrival of computers has made technical analysis both easier and more widely used. That doesn't mean that fundamental analysis is a useless dinosaur as a trading approach, but it does mean that even fundamental market analysts have to pay attention to technical factors that may be driving market prices.

Many traders use some combination of fundamental and technical Analysis. For example, a stock trader might select companies to Invest in based on fundamental analysis of market sectors and Various companies but select specific price entry and exit points Based on technical analysis.

TECHNICAL ANALYSIS IN DETAIL :

This is not a definitive science, rather a probabilistic discipline. In simple terms, it is more of an art than science. There are well known chart patterns or indicators in the market. But nothing works 100% of the time. We still follow them because they work more number of times than they fail. Hence emerged the concept of probability, the number of times anything works among the number of times that occur. With experience, a chartist is able to form an opinion of his or her own so that he has some extra edge on the market assessment than someone having just bookish knowledge of technical analysis. We request you to go through the concept slowly one at a time and keep observing charts on a regular basis. Look at old charts and look at contemporary live charts. Once you find a pattern or some indicators try to predict the future move and note down your prediction. Then as time flows try to match the price action with your prediction. Then analyse why it worked or not worked. Make notes and progress with the e-book and the notes. This is a long journey and we wish you best of luck.

Types of Charts:

Charts are two-dimensional representations of price over time. There are many types of charts available. But most popular and widely used among them are Line Charts, Bar Charts and the Candlestick Charts. The X axis, i.e. the time axis is crucial. The unit can be month, week, day, hour, 5 min or few seconds. The shorter the time period, the more detailed the chart becomes. Generally higher the time frame of the chart, relatively higher is the probability of any concept in the market.

- *Line Charts:*

In the line chart each price point is represented as a dot. The X axis represents the time scale and the Y axis represents the price. Each dot or point represents the closing price at the end of a unit of time. These points are then joined to form a line.

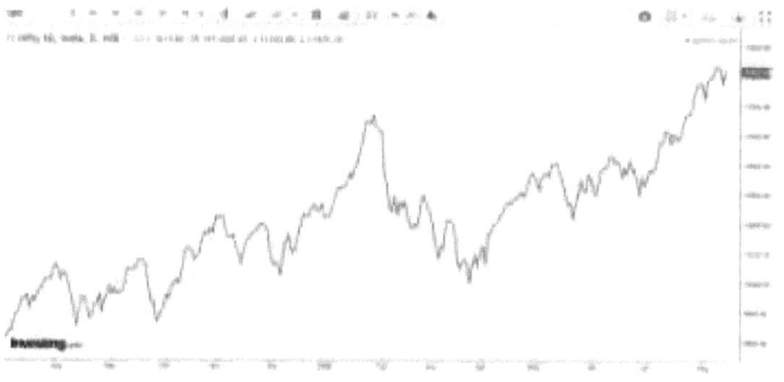

Figure: Line Chartaption

- *Bar Charts:*

A bar chart consists of a series of bars. Every bar has four important price points - open, close, high and low. The bars are represented in green or blue colour when close is higher than open and red colour when close is lower than open. The bar charts are more detailed than the line chart and are good for demonstrating or spotting the classical price patterns.

Figure: Bar Chart

•

Candlestick Chart (Widely Used):

The concept of candlestick charts came from Japan. That is why they are often referred to as Japanese candlestick charts. These charts are the most versatile and popular form of chart representation. Price behaviour during each time unit is represented in the form of a candle. If the closing price of a stock is higher than open price during a particular time period, then the candle is green, if the close price is below the open price then the candle is red. Each candle has a body and two wicks. The distance between open to close is represented by the body of a candle and the upper and lower wicks represent the highs and lows of a candle.

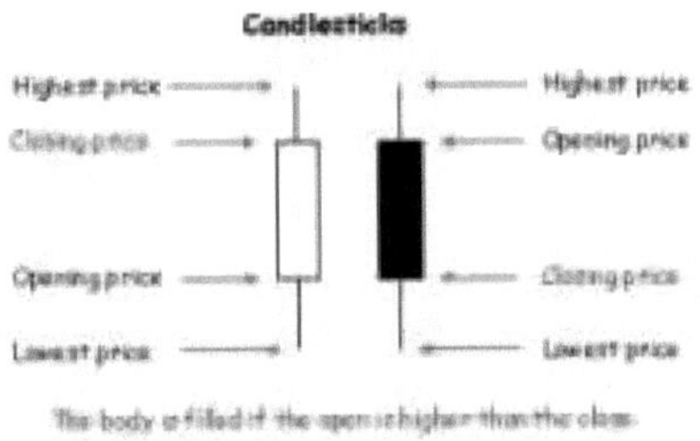

Figure: Candlestick

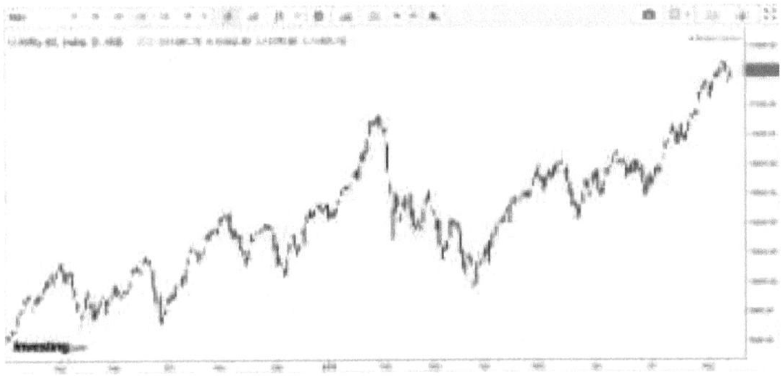

Figure: Candlestick Chart Diagrammatic Representation

Candlestick chart is special not only because it adds a special visual clarity about the price action, but also because often a single candlestick or two or three consecutive candlesticks together form a pattern that indicate reversal of a prior move or give conviction on continuation of the ongoing move. These are called candlestick patterns. We will discuss them later.

Trends:

Market Trend and Range-Bound Consolidation: Often market movements happen in the form of trends. A price trend is a continuous or a directional price movement in upward or downward direction. We call them up -trend and down -trend respectively. Now if we look at price action in the market through charts, we will find that no price movement happens in a straight line. Suppose we are looking at a broader uptrend represented as primary move, we may find intermediate corrections represented as secondary trend and minor counter moves among the secondary moves represented as minor trend. This is how the market behaves generally in both the up and the down Trends.

Figure: Market Trends

Often an up- trend is represented in the form of a sequence of higher highs and higher lows. Similarly, a downtrend is represented as a sequence of lower lows and lower highs. A trend is said to reverse when the sequence is broken.

Figure: Trend Reversal

We should remember a simple point that the market is not trending all the time. Often the market consolidates within a small range and goes nowhere. Then suddenly it can break on the upside or downside.

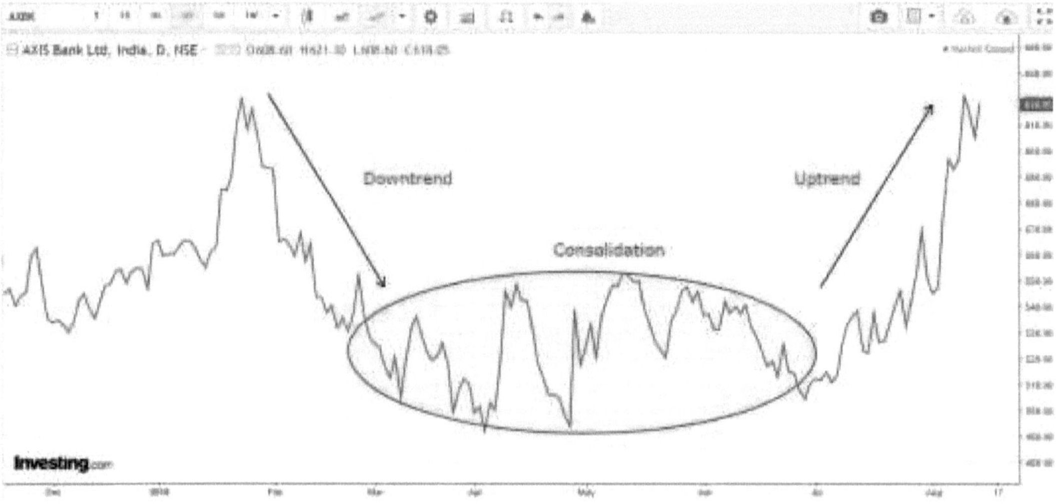

Figure: Downtrend Consolidation and Uptrend representation

Trendline & Channels:

Trendline and Channels are one of the most simple and useful tools in the market. During an uptrend, a trendline is formed by joining lowest points of periodic pullbacks, defined as secondary moves in the previous section. The uptrend line has a positive slope. To be precise we need two lows to join to form a trendline during an up-move. This line is then extended in the upward direction; the third move towards the trend-line is used to validate the trend line. If the trend line is not broken in the pull back, then it is called trend-line validation. It is often observed that price pulls back towards the trend line and moves higher. In an up-trending market, it is often easier to make money if one buys near the trend line and sells Higher.

Figure: Uptrend

Now when one buys, he or she is looking for the prices to move higher. But this may or may not happen. Hence the investor should maintain a stop loss point below which he-or she should cut his position, i.e. book loss. When a trend line is broken, either the market may reverse the trend, continue the uptrend with little less force or just go sideways.

Figure: Uptrend Reversal

Similarly, during a down-trend: a trendline is formed by joining pull- back highs. They slope downwards. Just like an up-trend line a down- trend line is formed by joining two points and then extended in downward direction. Pull backs towards the trend-lines are low risk points for short selling with a stop loss little above the trend line. More number of times the line is validated, the more it grows in importance.

Figure: Downtrend

Similar to an uptrend-line, when a down trending trend line is broken the trend may continue with less pace, or reverse or may go side-ways. A downward trend line is said to be an area of resistance.

Role Reversal:

Once a trendline support or resistance is broken, its role is reversed. If the price falls below a support line, that line will become resistance. If the price rises above a resistance line, it will often become support. For a true reversal to occur, however, it is important that the prices make a strong move through either the support or resistance line.

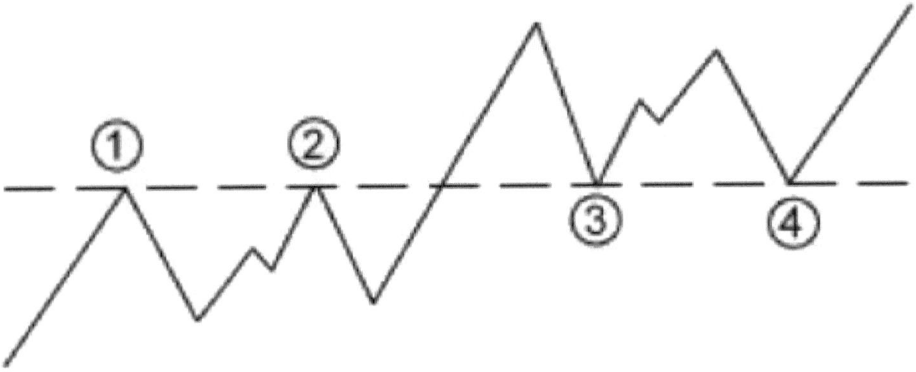

Figure: Role Reversal

Channels

The concept of the channel is much similar to trend lines. When in an uptrend or in a down trend or in a consolidation, we see rhythmic movement in the form of parallelogram, we can draw channels. The channel boundaries are good points for reversal trades with small stop losses. Once price is out of the channel, the trend or range of the stock is broken.

Figure: channel

Volume:

Traded volume is the number of quantities of stocks which change hands. The volume is shown as a sub graph in the price-time chart, below the price window. Higher the volume in any particular move, the greater is the conviction in that move to continue greater distance in that direction. However, if volume is on the lower side during a move, the stock is generally bound to lose momentum. Generally, during range bound phases, the volume is low.

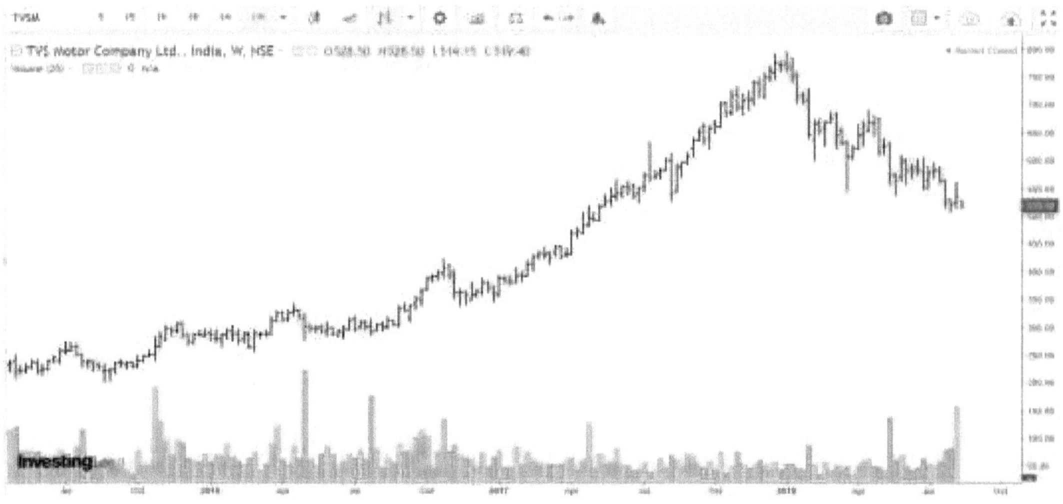

Figure : Volume

An important point regarding volume is that traded volume in absolute terms has no significance. When we talk about higher or lower volume, it is relative to average volume over certain time periods.

Trend Volume Interpretation: -

<u>*Trend Volume Interpretation*</u>

Up High Uptrend may go greater distance

Up Low Less conviction in the down move, may reverse

Down High Down move may cover greater distance

Down Low Less conviction in the down move, may reverse

Apart from traded volume, one important concept regarding volume is delivery %. In the market a person can first buy shares and sell by the end of the day. He or she can do the reverse too. This is called intra- day trading.

However, if an investor is having a positive view, he may buy the share and carry forward it for several days. This is called taking delivery of a share. Hence if there is a price rise of a stock with high % of delivery volume, then this signifies a positive conviction in the stock. If the supply is high and a lot of people look to sell the stock, then there are available buyers, the price is likely to decline. Hence a fall in price with high delivery % is known as negative for a stock.

- Classical Chart patterns: As we have discussed in the previous section, that market can be either in trending phase or in a range- bound phase. No trend generally lasts forever in the market. After prolonged or medium or shorter duration up and downtrend, the market often reverses, and a move starts in the opposite direction of the prior move. Often, we find that well defined geometrical patterns are formed in the chart which provides good indication of price reversals. These patterns are called reversal classical chart patterns.

We will discuss a few of the classical chart patterns in the following section.

Head and Shoulder & Inverse Head & Shoulder:

- Head and Shoulder pattern is a bearish reversal pattern. This pattern appears after an uptrend. This pattern is formed with three consecutive tops with the middle one being higher than the other two. The middle top is called the head and the two side peaks are called the shoulders. On joining the intermediate troughs, we get the neckline. On ultimate break below the neckline, usually a short trade is taken with a stop-loss above the top of the nearest shoulder.

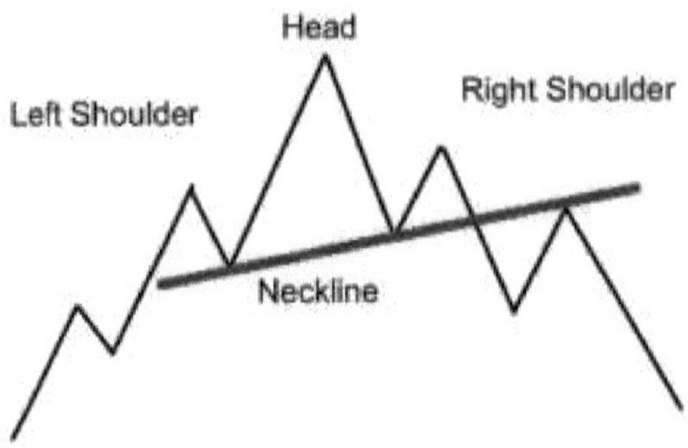

Figure : Head and Shoulder Pattern

- An Inverse Head and Shoulder is just a mirror image of the Head and Shoulder pattern. This should appear after a sustained down trend; the rule of stop loss and target are similar. This often acts as a very effective bullish reversal pattern.

Double Tops and Bottoms:

- These chart patterns are well-known patterns that signal a trend reversal – these are considered to be one of the most reliable patterns and are commonly used. These patterns are formed after a sustained trend and signal to chartists that the trend is about to reverse. These patterns are created when price movement tests support or resistance levels twice and is unable to break through. These patterns are often used to signal intermediate and long-term trend reversals.

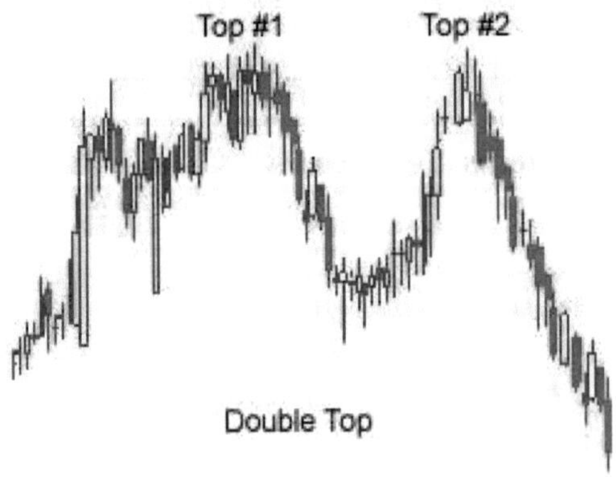

Figure : Double Top

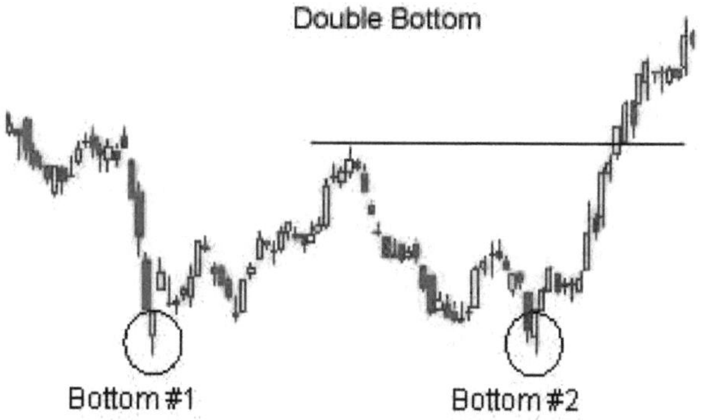

Figure : Double Bottom

Triple Tops and Bottoms:

- These are another set of reversal chart patterns in chart analysis. These two chart patterns are formed when the price movement tests a level of support or resistance three times and is unable to break through. They signal a reversal of the prior trend. A trade entry is initiated at the break of a neckline with a small stop-loss and the target is measured as the distance between peaks/troughs and the neckline.

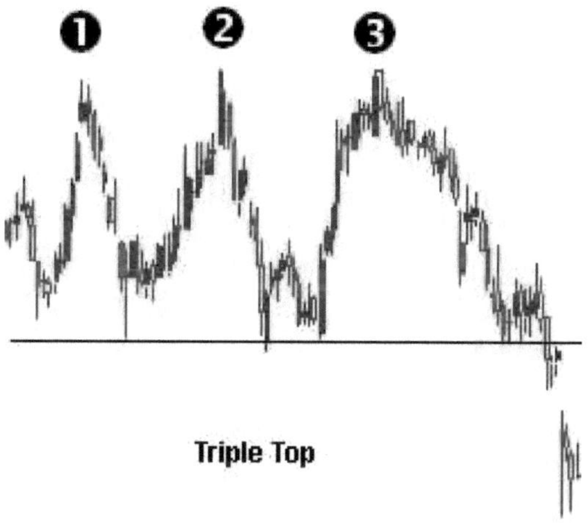

Figure : Tripple Top

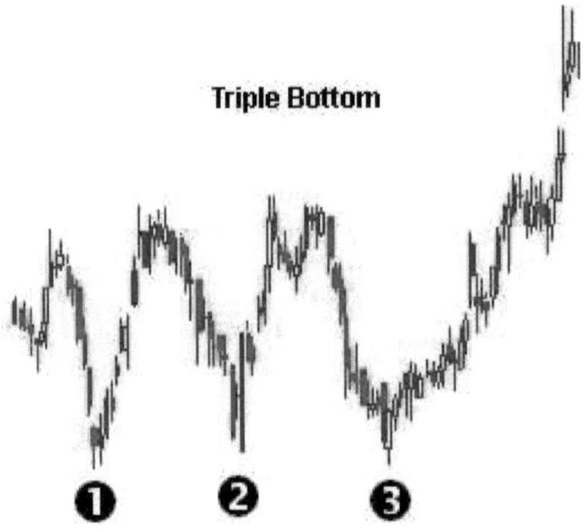

Figure : Tripple Bottom

Triangles:

- Triangles are one of the most well-known chart patterns used in technical analysis. The three most common types of triangles, which vary in construction and implications, are Symmetrical Triangle, Ascending Triangle and Descending Triangle. These chart patterns are considered to last anywhere from a couple of weeks (ideally more than 12 weeks) to several months. These are areas of consolidations after a trending move and are generally continuation patterns, i.e. the erstwhile trends resume after the breakout. However, in certain cases they act as reversal patterns. They can appear both in up-trend and down-trend.

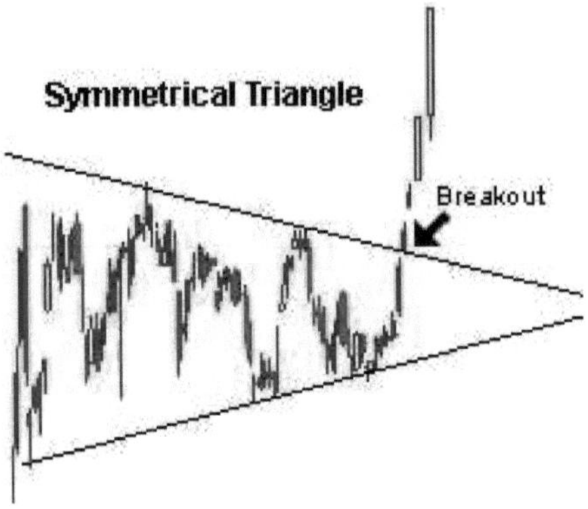

Figure : Symmetric Triangle

Figure : Ascending Triangle

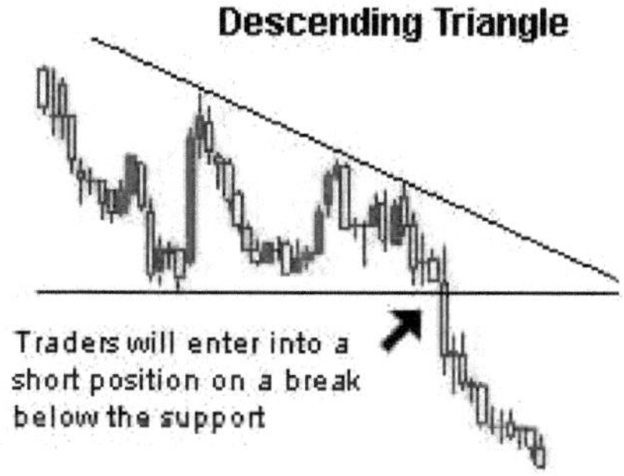

Figure : Descending Triangle

Flag and Pennant:

- These two short-term chart patterns are continuation patterns that are formed when there is a sharp price movement followed by a generally sideways price movement. They can appear both in up-trend and Down-trend.

Figure : Flag Pattern

Figure : Pennant

Candlestick Reversal Patterns:

When we had discussed about the candlestick charts, we had said that they have an edge over many other types of charts representation due to recognizable chart patterns which are easy to define and which work beautifully in the market. In this section we will discuss a few chart popular candlestick patterns. Candlestick patterns provide entry and stop- loss criteria, but there is no target setup as available in classical chart patterns.

- *Hammer:*

Hammer is a single candlestick bullish reversal pattern. This occurs after a prolonged down trend. The candle formed in this process should have a small body, a big lower shadow and a negligibly small upper shadow. Ideally the lower shadow should be at least twice the length of the body. The colour of the body can be either green or red, but if the body colour is green, then the hammer is considered a little more bullish, as the bulls were strong enough to close the price higher than the open price. The next day or in the next two or three days, ideally the price should move above the high of the hammer candle. This is called confirmation or validation of the pattern. A hammer like candle, without validation has no real significance. If price moves above the high of the hammer a buy trade can be taken with a stop loss below the low of the candle.

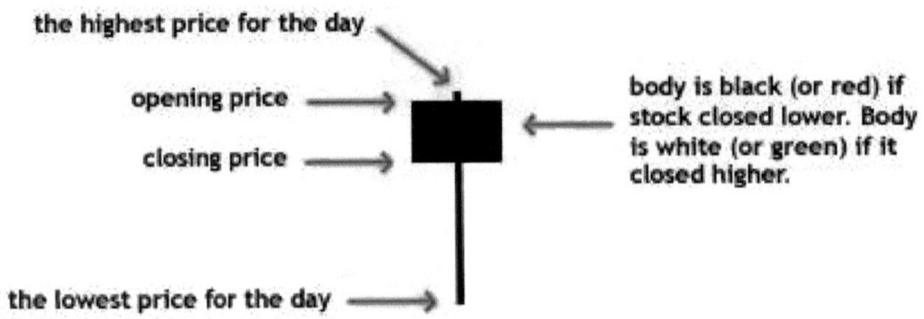

Figure : Hammer

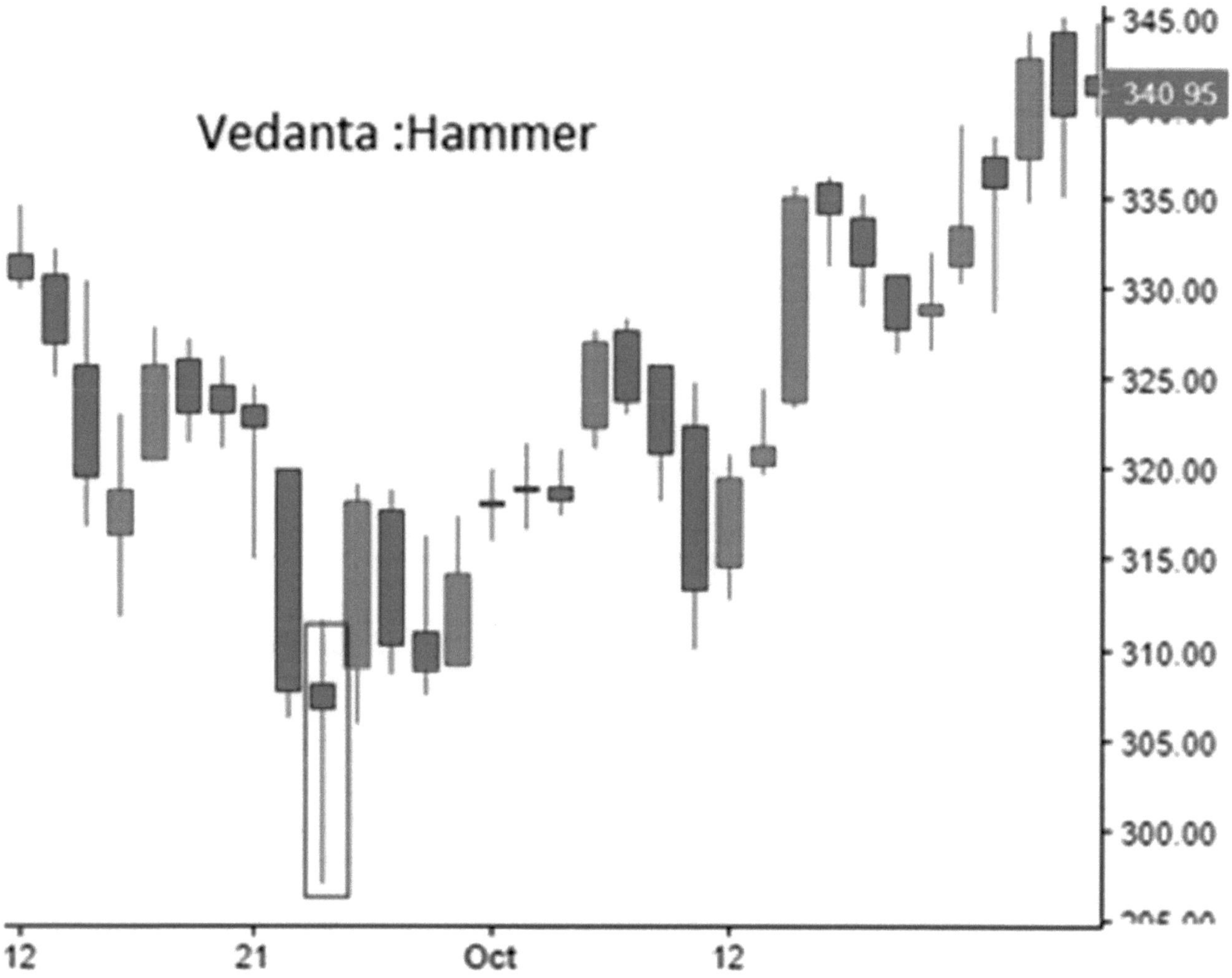

Figure : Hammer Example

•

Shooting Star:

A shooting star is just like a mirror image of a hammer candle. First there should be a sustained up trend and eventually the closing price should be very close to the opening price, resulting in a candle with a small green or red body, a big upper shadow and a small or negligible lower shadow. The upper shadow of the candle should be at least twice the length of the body. Now a confirmation of the shooting star pattern comes if price moves below the low of the candle within the next 2-3 candles. On confirmation, a short trade should be taken with stop loss above the high of the high of the candle. A shooting star pattern with a red body is considered slightly more bearish than one with a green body. It is often observed that shooting star candlestick pattern acts as bearish reversal pattern and triggers a down move after an uptrend.

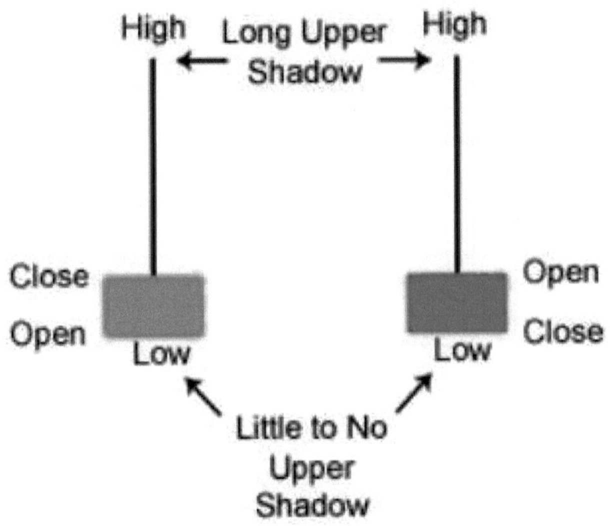

Figure: Shooting Star

- *Inverted-Hammer:*

An inverted hammer is a single candlestick bullish reversal pattern. The pattern appears after a sustained downtrend. The resulting candle should have a small body, red or green, the upper wick should be at least twice the body of the candle and the lower shadow should be quite small or negligible in size. If the body is green it is relatively more bullish than if it is red. This looks like an inverted hammer as the name suggests. The philosophy is that bears were not able to push the price below the opening price during the course of the day. This pattern, however, is considered to be little less bullish than the hammer itself, because in hammer bulls are able to force a higher close by the end of the day. The confirmation of the pattern comes once the price moves above the high of the candle. On confirmation a buy trade can be initiated with a stop loss below the low of the candle.

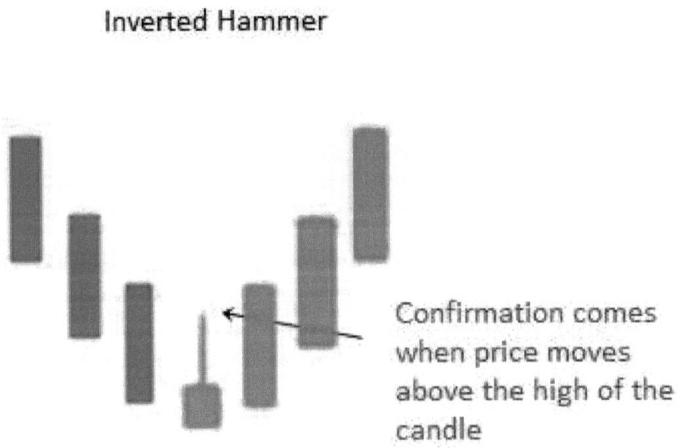

Figure: Inverted Hammer

- *Hanging Man:*

Hanging Man is a single candlestick bearish reversal pattern. This appears after a sustained up-move. The candle looks like a hammer; the only difference is that it appears at the end of an up-trend. The candle should have a small body at the top (red/green) and a lower shadow at least twice the length of the body. There should be very small or no upper shadow. A red coloured hanging man pattern is more bearish than a hanging man pattern with a green body. The confirmation of the pattern happens when price moves below the low of the candle. On confirmation a trader may take short trade with stop-loss above the high of the candle.

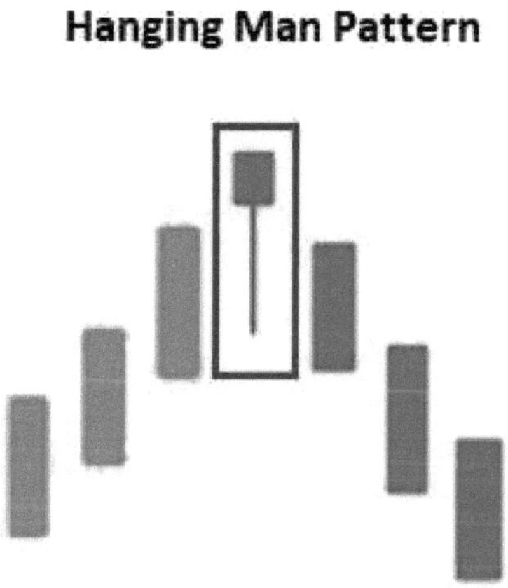

Figure: Hanging Man Pattern

- *Bullish Engulfing Pattern:*

Bullish candlestick pattern is a two- candlestick bullish reversal pattern. First there should be a downtrend. Then we should have a red candle followed by a green candle. The body of the green candle should engulf the body of the first red candle. If the highest point of these two candlesticks is breached on the upside within the next 2-3 candles, the bearish engulfing pattern is said to be confirmed. A buy trade can be initiated upon confirmation with stop-loss below the low of the two candlestick patterns.

Figure: Bullish Engulfing Pattern

•

Bearish Engulfing Pattern:

Bearish Engulfing pattern is just a mirror image of a bullish engulfing pattern with bearish implication. First, we should be having an up-trend. Then we should have a green candle as a continuation. The 2nd day candle should eventually close red with its body totally engulfing the body of the first candle. The confirmation comes when within the next 2-3 candles the price moves below the low of the two candles forming the Bearish Engulfing pattern. On confirmation a trader may take a short trade with stop loss above the top of the two candlestick patterns. Larger the 2nd candle, the more bearish the pattern.

Figure: Bearish Engulfing Pattern

•

Doji:

The Doji is a single candlestick pattern. The Doji assumes significance, when it appears after a trending move, be it up or down. The Doji symbolizes indecision and after a Doji the incumbent trend can reverse, go sideways or continue uptrend. However, the appearance of a Doji is a signal of caution that the probability is high that the erstwhile trend may be coming to an end. Doji is a candle which has open and close almost at a similar level. There can be upper shadows and lower shadows of various proportions.

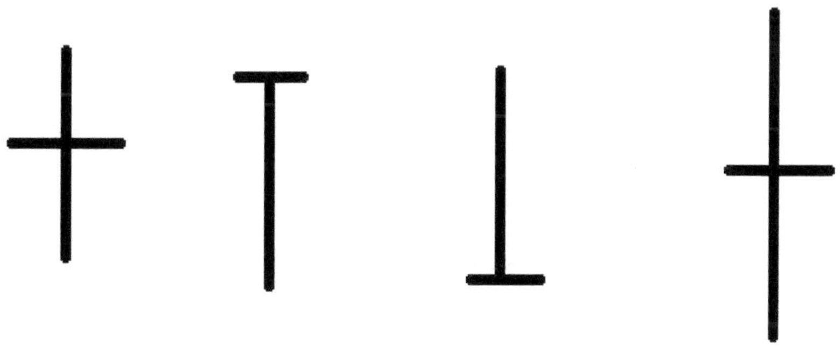

Figure: Doji

Indicators:

Indicators are tools to aid decision making in the market. There are various types of indicators which measure or indicate the trend, the momentum, the volatility and various other aspects in the market. There are thousands of indicators which are derived out of the price and volume data over time. Here we introduce you with two very useful indicators.

- ### *Simple Moving Average:*

Simple Moving Average or SMA is a moving average which is calculated by adding the closing price of security prices for the last n-periods and dividing it by the total number of time periods.

For example, suppose we want to calculate the 9 periods SMA of a security price.

First, we will add the last 9 Days Closing Price of the security and then it will be divided by the 9 periods. Calculation for 9 periods SMA: (P9+P8+P7+P6.... +P1)/9

Where, P=Price

P9= Closing Price 9 days ago

SMA is a Technical indicator which is represented by a line and it is directly plotted on the security price. As per the choice of the trader, the periods can be changed in the SMA Indicator.

For shorter-term SMA, we can use 5,8,13 etc. For Medium term 20, 34, 50 and for longer term 100,200 can be used.

If a medium-term moving average is having a positive slope, the trend is considered to be positive in the medium term and vice versa.

Price breaching a particular moving average from down to up is considered a bullish sign. Similarly, price breaching a particular moving average from upside and closing below is considered bearish. If we find a shorter-term moving average crossing a medium-term moving average from below, often this is called bullish crossover. On the other hand, if a shorter term moving average crosses a medium-term moving average from upside to below that is called a bearish crossover and often considered a signal of bearishness.

Figure: Simple Moving Average

•

RSI:

Relative Strength Index (RSI) is a momentum oscillator, developed by J. Welles Wilder, which measures the speed and velocity of price movement of trading instruments (stocks, commodity futures, bonds, forex etc.) over a specified period of time.

The objective of the RSI indicator is to measure the change in price momentum. It is a leading indicator and is widely used by Technical Analysts over the globe. RSI can be used to spot a general trend. It is considered overbought when it goes above 70 and oversold when it goes below 30.

The 30-70 region of RSI is considered to be a normal zone.

The formula for calculating Relative Strength Index is as follows RSI = 100 – 100 / (1 + RS)

RS = Average Gain over specified period/ Average loss over the same period

The default setting for Relative Strength Index is 14, but you may change this value to decrease or increase sensitivity based on your requirement.

Usage: There are many kinds of usage of RSI. However, most popularly, if we find that, RSI breaching the 70 level and at the same time we spot a bearish reversal pattern, then there is opportunity to take short trade with stop loss. Similarly, if RSI breaches 30 from below and we observe a bullish reversal pattern, there is opportunity to take long trade with stop loss.

Figure: Relative Strength Index

conclusion

Ideally traders combine indicators and price patterns to form their trading strategies. Very rarely professional traders just rely on a single indicator or a price pattern. We are about to end our short journey of introducing you with the concept of basic charting. Hope this gives you enough clarity and generates great interest in your mind to apply those concepts in live charts. Technical analysis is a discipline in which a practitioner improves and learns with time and practice. We wish you all the best in your journey.

Printed by Libri Plureos GmbH in Hamburg,
Germany

9 798889 594437